Safety First!

Safety on the Internet

by Lucia Raatma

Consultant:
Lawrence J. Magid
Editor-in-Chief
SafeKids.Com and SafeTeens.Com

Bridgestone Books
an imprint of Capstone Press
Mankato, Minnesota

Bridgestone Books are published by Capstone Press
818 North Willow Street, Mankato, Minnesota 56001
http://www.capstone-press.com

Library of Congress Cataloging-in-Publication Data
Safety on the Internet/by Lucia Raatma.
p. cm.—(Safety first!)
Includes bibliographical references and index.
Summary: An introduction to the Internet and how to use it safely.
ISBN 0-7368-0192-8
1. Internet (Computer network) and children—United States—Juvenile literature.
2. Internet (Computer network)—Security measures—United States—Juvenile literature.
3. Computer networks—Access control—United States—Juvenile literature. [1. Internet
(Computer network)—Safety measures. 2. Safety.] I. Title. II. Series: Raatma, Lucia. Safety first!
HQ784.I58R33 1999
025.04—dc21   98-45325
                                                                                          CIP
                                                                                          AC

Editorial Credits
Rebecca Glaser, editor; Steve Christensen, cover designer; Linda Clavel, illustrator; Kimberly
    Danger, photo researcher

Photo Credits
David F. Clobes, 6, 10, 16, 18, 20
PhotoBank, Inc./Bill Lai, cover; Gary A. Conner, 4 (bottom), 14 (bottom right)
Photophile/Ceniceros, 4 (top)
Unicorn Stock Photos/Karen Helsinger Mulien, 14 (bottom left); A. Ramey I, 14 (top right); Steve
    Bourgeois, 14 (top left)

Search engine shown on page 12 used by permission of Ask Jeeves, Inc., Berkeley, CA, copyright Ask Jeeves,
Inc., 1997–1998, all rights reserved. Ask Jeeves for Kids is a trademark of Ask Jeeves, Inc.

Netscape browser and e-mail frames on pages 8 and 12 used by permission. Netscape Communications
Corporation has not authorized, sponsored, endorsed, or approved this publication and is not responsible for
its content. Netscape and the Netscape Communications Corporate logos are trademarks and trade names of
Netscape Communications Corporation. All other product names and/or logos are trademarks of their
respective owners.

Table of Contents

The Internet

The Internet connects your computer to computers around the world. You can write to friends and learn new facts. But strangers also use the Internet. And some Internet sites are only for adults. You can learn to be safe on the Internet.

Internet site

a place on the Internet with facts, games, or pictures

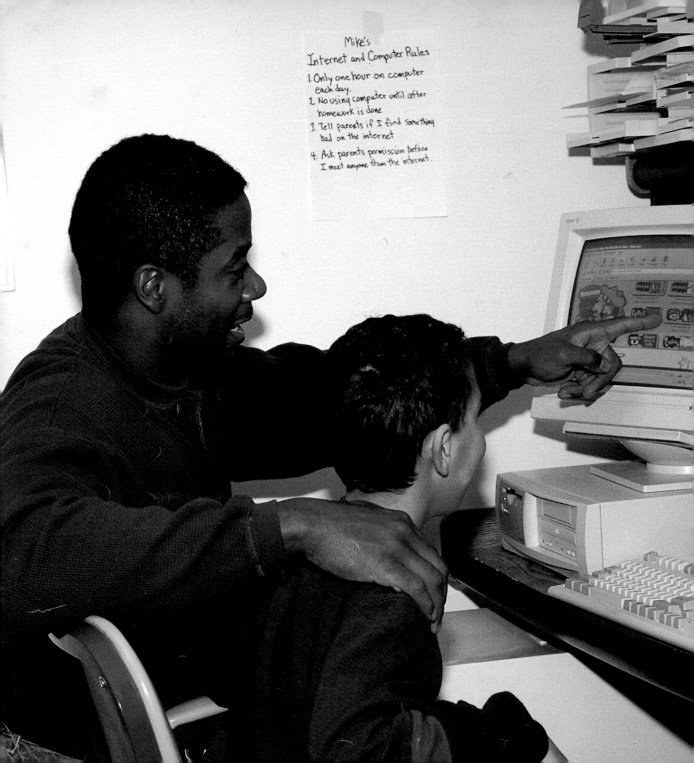

Mike's
Internet and Computer Rules

1. Only one hour on computer each day.
2. No using computer until after homework is done
3. Tell parents if I find something bad on the internet
4. Ask parents permission before I meet anyone from the internet.

Internet Rules

Talk to your parents about rules for using the Internet. They may suggest a time limit for you. They may set up rules for the kinds of Internet sites you can use. They may tell you not to give out your phone number and address.

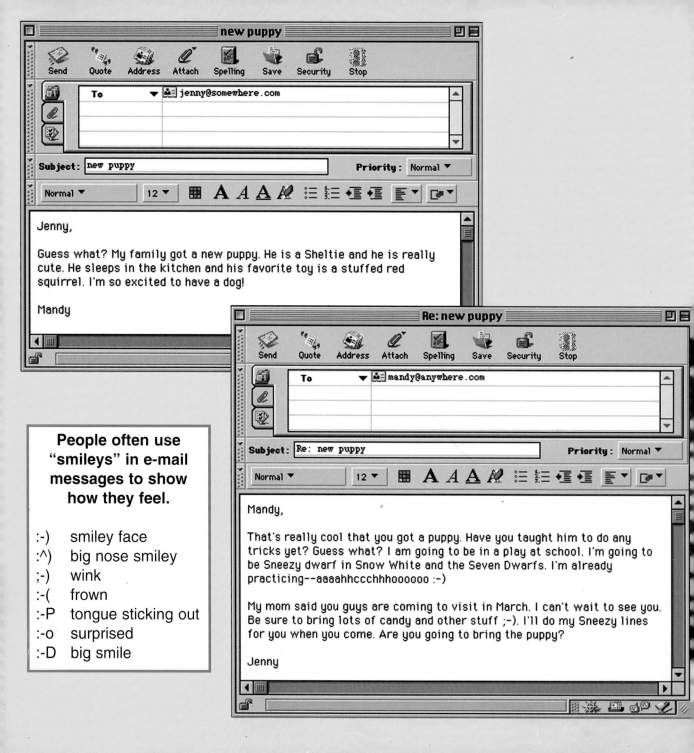

new puppy

Send Quote Address Attach Spelling Save Security Stop

To ▼ 📇 jenny@somewhere.com

Subject: new puppy   Priority: Normal ▼

Normal ▼ 12 ▼

Jenny,

Guess what? My family got a new puppy. He is a Sheltie and he is really cute. He sleeps in the kitchen and his favorite toy is a stuffed red squirrel. I'm so excited to have a dog!

Mandy

Re: new puppy

Send Quote Address Attach Spelling Save Security Stop

To ▼ 📇 mandy@anywhere.com

Subject: Re: new puppy   Priority: Normal ▼

Normal ▼ 12 ▼

Mandy,

That's really cool that you got a puppy. Have you taught him to do any tricks yet? Guess what? I am going to be in a play at school. I'm going to be Sneezy dwarf in Snow White and the Seven Dwarfs. I'm already practicing--aaaahhcccchhhoooooo :-)

My mom said you guys are coming to visit in March. I can't wait to see you. Be sure to bring lots of candy and other stuff ;-). I'll do my Sneezy lines for you when you come. Are you going to bring the puppy?

Jenny

People often use "smileys" in e-mail messages to show how they feel.

:-)   smiley face
:^)   big nose smiley
;-)   wink
:-(frown
:-P   tongue sticking out
:-o   surprised
:-D   big smile

Safety with E-Mail

E-mail lets you send and receive letters over the Internet. Be careful if you get e-mail from a stranger. Show an adult. Do not write back to a stranger. Some people send links to Internet sites through e-mail. Do not click on these links without your parents' permission.

link
a colored word, underlined word, or graphic that will take you to another Internet site when you click on it

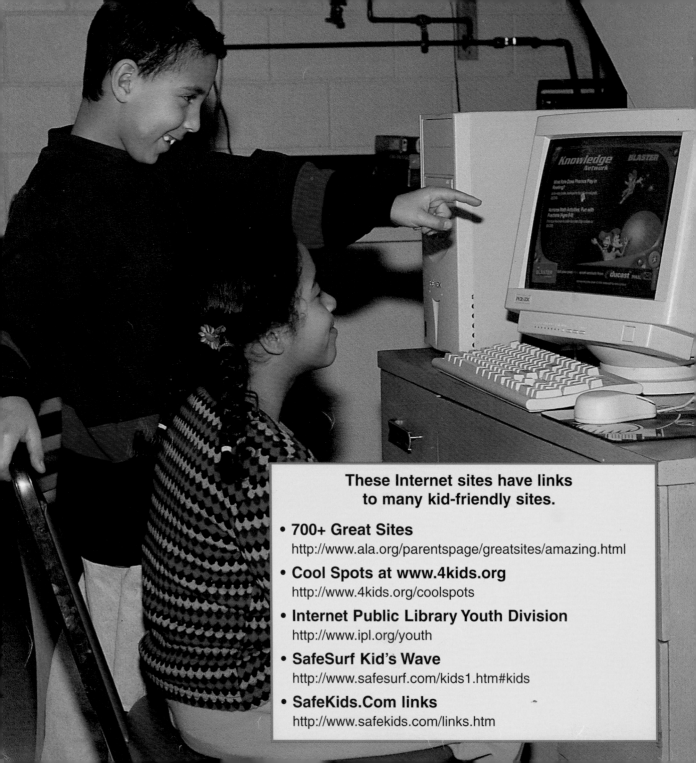

**These Internet sites have links
to many kid-friendly sites.**

- **700+ Great Sites**
  http://www.ala.org/parentspage/greatsites/amazing.html
- **Cool Spots at www.4kids.org**
  http://www.4kids.org/coolspots
- **Internet Public Library Youth Division**
  http://www.ipl.org/youth
- **SafeSurf Kid's Wave**
  http://www.safesurf.com/kids1.htm#kids
- **SafeKids.Com links**
  http://www.safekids.com/links.htm

Safety with Internet Sites

Some Internet sites tell you about faraway places. Other sites have games to play or offer homework help. But some Internet sites are only for adults. These sites are not right for kids. Tell an adult if you find this type of site.

11

These search engines find sites just for kids.

Ask Jeeves for Kids!
http://ajkids.com

Super Snooper
http://www.supersnooper.com/

Disney's Internet Guide
http://www.disney.com/dig/today/

Yahooligans!
http://www.yahooligans.com

Safety with Search Engines

Search engines find many sites about a subject. For example, you could type "baseball." The search engine will list sites about baseball. But sometimes these searches find sites that are only for adults. Use search engines that find sites that are safe for kids.

```
<JAYBIRD_08> Hi
<SK8BORDER> Hi
<LUV2SWIM_f/10> Anyone here from North
 Carolina?
<JAYBIRD_08> I'm from South Carolina
<Nrthnlites> Anyone here from Alaska?
<LUV2SWIM_f/10> Where in SC?
<JAYBIRD_08> Walterboro
<SK8BORDER> Is MONSTER9 here?
<Nrthnlites> Who's MONSTER9?
<JAYBIRD_08> Just left
<LUV2SWIM_f/10> A surfer from Texas
<SK8BORDER> Is it cold in AK?
<JAYBIRD_08> LUV2SWIM Where are you from
 in NC?
<Nrthnlites> Yeah
<LUV2SWIM_f/10> Fayetteville
<MONSTER9> I'm back. What's up?
```

Safety in Chat Rooms

You can meet people and talk about your favorite hobbies in chat rooms. But you can never be sure who is in a chat room. Ask an adult before entering a chat room. Never give out your real name. Leave the chat room if someone there makes you nervous.

chat room

a place on the Internet where several people type messages at one time; some chat rooms cover one subject or age group.

Strangers on the Internet

It is safe to talk and write to most people on the Internet. But you cannot hear or see them. People might not be who they say they are. Never give a stranger your name, phone number, or address. Tell an adult if anyone bothers you on the Internet.

Meeting People from the Internet

You and a keypal may want to meet in person. Ask a parent before you agree to meet anyone. Meet in a public place if a parent says it is OK. It is very important that you do not go alone. Ask your parent to go with you.

keypal
a friend on the Internet; keypals write e-mail letters to each other.

When to Log Off

The Internet can be fun. But remember
to follow the rules your parents set. Log
off when your time limit is up. Log off
if someone makes you nervous or uses
bad language. You can be safe if you
remember these rules.

log off

to turn off your Internet service

Hands On: Using Search Engines for Kids

Many Internet sites are helpful and fun. But they can be hard to find. Use search engines made just for kids.

What You Need
A computer with Internet access

What You Do
1. Choose one of the search engines listed on page 12. Type in the Internet address on your computer.
2. What hobbies or subjects do you want to learn more about? Type in your word and click "Search." The search engine will give you a list of sites.
3. You will find sites faster if you use exact words. The word "dogs" will bring up hundreds of sites. But if you type "golden retrievers" or "terriers," you will find sites about those types of dogs.
4. Some search engines let you type in questions. For example, you might ask, "What is the capital of Spain?"
5. Some sites have links to other sites for kids. You can click on these pictures or underlined words to go to other sites.

Words to Know

chat room (CHAT ROOM)—a place on the Internet where several people type messages at one time; some chat rooms cover one subject or age group.

e-mail (EE-mayl)—electronic letters sent over the Internet; most e-mail arrives in a few minutes.

keypal (KEE-pal)—a friend you write to on the Internet

link (LINGK)—a colored word, underlined word, or graphic on an Internet site that will take you to another Internet site when you click on it

log off (LOG OFF)—to turn off your Internet service

site (SITE)—a place on the Internet with facts, games, or pictures

Read More

Brimner, Larry Dane. *E-Mail.* A True Book. New York: Children's Press, 1997.

Kazunas, Charnan and Tom. *The Internet for Kids.* A True Book. New York: Children's Press, 1997.

Internet Sites

Kid Safety on the Internet—The Police Notebook
http://www.ou.edu/oupd/kidsafe/inet.htm
My Rules for Online Safety
http://www.safekids.com/myrules.htm
Safety Tips for Kids on the Internet
http://www.fbi.gov/kids/internet/internet.htm

Index